Modern Order

HOUSES BY ROBERT GURNEY

Introduction by Vernon Mays | Edited by Carolyn Horwitz

First published in the United States of America by
Architecture/Interiors Press, Inc.
4455 Los Feliz Boulevard, Suite 106
Los Angeles, California 90027 USA
www.architectureinteriorspress.com

ISBN: 978-0-9823190-1-7
Library of Congress Control Number: 2009925191

Designed by Matthew Papa
Edited by Carolyn Horwitz

Modern Order by Vernon Mays

Robert Gurney was designing modern houses long before modern was cool—or at least, cool in Washington, DC. That fact isn't attributable to Gurney's status as an early pioneer of modernism with decades of seasoning—he's far too young for that label. Rather, the distinction has more to do with the fact that establishment Washington tends to follow, not lead, when it comes to matters of fashion, art, and architecture.

So, at the time Gurney was breaking into architecture in the mid-1980s, the prevailing demand was for houses that looked familiar: roofs with gables, windows with shutters, siding made of brick or clapboard—certainly not façades composed of vast sheets of glass neatly trimmed with metal. As the '80s progressed, the rising tide of postmodernism did little to give an aspiring modernist architect a sense of buoyancy. But Gurney is an optimist at heart, and so he did what he could to satisfy his clients with houses that were informed by a modernist spirit.

After launching a small office in 1990 in Alexandria, Virginia, Gurney survived on primarily small additions. One such project was a revamped kitchen and spacious new family room that fit well in its northwest Washington neighborhood, with exterior flourishes such as a hipped roof, cupola, and moon-shaped weather vane. Inside, however, the addition boasts abundant natural light, free-flowing space, and clever built-in cabinets concealing a large entertainment center.

Breakthroughs began in the late '90s. Gurney's addition to a Lovettsville, Virginia, farmhouse set itself apart: The deep-red board-and-batten siding and enclosed staircase projecting outside the volume of the addition clearly signaled that something was up—something beyond the ordinary. Finally, by the turn of the century, an influx of new money and the impact of national media (from shelter magazines to home-conscious reality TV shows) had enhanced the appetite for modern design among Washingtonians. Breaking the cultural inertia of the old-money set was an influx of young people who eschewed traditional houses.

Gurney's patience had paid off. At last he was able to build what he envisioned: contemporary houses that are ordered, rigorous, functional, and light-filled. And unlike many mid-century modern houses—whose interiors can be stark in their simplicity—there's a palpable sensuality to Gurney's handling of materials inside the shell of the building.

His infatuation with elegant materials and overlapping spaces conceals the fact that Gurney first came to understand buildings in a gritty sort of way. His father, a New York City firefighter, had a second job as bricklayer. From the time he was 10 years old, Gurney labored at his father's side, mixing

cement and carrying bricks. By the time he was a young architect, tackling two successive Capitol Hill rowhouses early in his career, Gurney had developed a deep knowledge of how buildings go together. "I'd do the demolition, I'd do the framing, I'd do the drywall," he explains. "When you do everything yourself, you learn so much." But the benefits of getting his hands dirty went deeper than construction know-how. The experience helped Gurney develop a sensitivity for the way materials feel, in addition to how they look—a tactility that is expressed in his buildings as compositions of textures.

In his Packard Komoriya Residence, for example, Gurney achieved unity with the surrounding woods and rock outcroppings by weaving a rich tapestry of natural materials into a house defined by crisp angles and clarity of form. On the exterior, muted colors are a foil to the rich variety of textures revealed by closer inspection—rugged dry-stacked stone, gold-flecked cedar shingles, and striated board-formed concrete. Inside, there is a shift to the smooth and elegant: Brazilian cherry floors, maple cabinetry and paneling, and steel railings with the finish of German machine parts.

Gurney's career has been largely self-directed. Unlike many architects, he didn't latch on to a mentor whose methods he studied and whose aesthetic preferences he adopted. Instead, he devoured books and design journals. Outside of work, he and his wife soaked up design culture wherever they could—attending lectures in the District, visiting significant new buildings, taking vacations to look at buildings and art. "I loved that aspect of it," he enthuses.

Consequently, his influences are diverse. Rather than following the lead of a single architect, he tracks the latest and greatest work of an eclectic range of modernists. His tastes range from the restrained palette of mid-century modernists to the more willful, form-based work of contemporary designers. Even a flair for the sophisticated minimalism found more often in New York and London emerges in some of Gurney's retail showrooms and urban developments, such as the Ontario Apartment in Washington. "There are different clients, different projects, different programs that warrant different solutions," he explains. "I don't think you apply one aesthetic way of solving a problem to every project. That diversity is fun."

One method Gurney uses to avoid the trap of sameness is to let his process be his guide. When asked how he starts to hatch a design, he fires back an immediate answer: "It's the site. For new houses on a freestanding property, the site drives everything." One informative example is the Kessler Residence in Chevy Chase, Maryland, which occupies the middle of a comfortably scaled domestic

block. In deference to the neighborhood, Gurney's first step was to construct a prototypical house form on the front of the lot—a kind of exaggerated Monopoly house, with broad openings and a steeply pitched roof. Behind it, a flat-roofed pavilion houses a sunny living/dining/kitchen suite on the ground floor and a luxurious master bedroom suite above. The hybrid solution resulted in one of Gurney's most successful residential works, exuding elegance, warmth, versatility, and a mature hand.

Another illustrative example of the importance of site, quite different in outcome, is the Blue Ridge Farmhouse on the outskirts of picturesque Washington, Virginia. Gurney was invited to build an addition to a well-proportioned, clapboard residence that stands sentry over a 500-acre farm with idyllic vistas of the Blue Ridge Mountains. He recalls walking around the house and finding a comfortable spot on the back lawn. "I thought, 'If I just put a roof over my head, this would be the most beautiful space in the world,' " he recalls. The ultimate design wasn't nearly that simplistic—it is, in fact, a dexterous play of solids and voids—but the broad stroke of making a glass pavilion from which to best appreciate the magnificent vistas stemmed from that experience of the place.

Once he has grappled with site conditions, Gurney turns his attention to the functional program. He organizes it in purely spatial terms; ie., three bedrooms, two baths, living room, office, bowling alley, swimming pool—whatever the case may be. At the same time, he explores the clients' lifestyle. Do they entertain informally, with formal gatherings a few times per year? What is their typical daily schedule? He factors in budget, then combines all these criteria into an initial sketch or model. Never does he enter a project with a preconceived notion of what he's going to design.

Even after the idea begins to take shape, he resists the temptation to mold the house into a single object, preferring instead to render the major program elements as individual spaces and volumes that serve a purpose. Gurney's desire to make all the spaces feel different is clearly reflected in projects such as the Hargrave Residence and Occoquan River House, in which the primary spaces are articulated with varying ceiling heights that, by extension, create compositions of independent volumes.

The purposefulness of that approach is clarified by the small axonometric drawings that accompany each of the case studies in this book. Through them, Gurney illustrates the artful, compositional strategy that pervades his design method. Like giant still-life paintings rendered at the scale of the street, his houses are careful arrangements of shapes that give individuality and clarity to the main elements of the residential program. Sometimes he takes the game a step further by modifying the roof forms; often he creates additional distinctions by varying the exterior materials.

When it comes to interiors, materials are paramount. In Gurney's design approach, the interior finishes are much less about selecting fabrics and paint colors than about creating meaningful articulations of texture and surface. Colorful, hand-finished plasters, natural stone, oxidized metal, warm-stained woods, and ground-face concrete block are frequently found inside Gurney's houses. In some cases, the interest is heightened by using the materials in unusual ways. For instance, in the Fitch O'Rourke Residence, for which Gurney won a national Honor Award in 2001 from the American Institute of Architects, rolling metal frames that offer privacy to the upper-level rooms are clad in copper wire cloth that is intended for industrial use as conveyor belts or in agricultural filtration equipment. The use of wire cloth as a privacy screen is appropriate because of its translucency, but the material also possesses a glistening quality that elevates it from the mundane.

It's no accident that the interiors of Gurney's projects maintain a consistent level of excellence and sophistication, and he is quick to credit his long-time critic, companion, collaborator, and wife, Thérèse Baron Gurney, for her contributions in this regard. An interior designer who refined her craft while working in the office of Hugh Newell Jacobsen, Thérèse plays a vital role in all of her husband's projects—whether functioning as a sounding board or taking the lead on furniture selection.

Ultimately, Gurney credits his clients with giving him the opportunities that produced the houses in this book. Although one shouldn't characterize his practice as a service firm—a term that can be taken as a backhanded compliment in the architectural profession—Gurney isn't hesitant to say that his goal is to please the client, rather than serve his own ambitions. "I am always open-minded to what my clients think," he says. "And I always tell my clients I'm never going to shoot down, without reason, anything they throw out to me. At the same time, they have to be open-minded to anything I present. I think that's a good way of doing it."

Collaboration, then, is a key ingredient in Gurney's work. It helps him discover the intangible things that separate a good house from a mediocre one. Questions from a client, a little prodding here and there, have a way of opening the architect's eyes to new possibilities. And Gurney says those conversations help him create the thing he pursues most insistently—a house that works. "You can't do something that's beautiful if it doesn't work," he insists. "And I like to think my projects are well-thought-out. They're ordered; they're organized. The stairs are in the right place, the bathroom is in the right place, the entrance is in the right place—they work. But like Le Corbusier always said, it has to be beautiful too." And nowadays—even if it's modern—that plays well around Washington, DC.

Buisson Residence

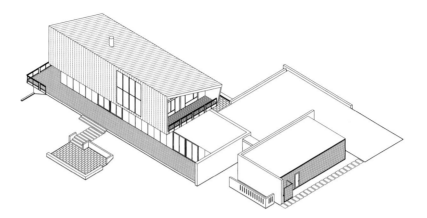

Buisson Residence Lake Anna, Virginia | 7,500 sq ft | 2008

Situated on a grass knoll and commanding views of Lake Anna in central Virginia, the Buisson Residence is reached via a road that winds through a pine forest. The house emerges in the form of a copper-clad volume cantilevered above a long, white brick wall.

The primary organizational elements are two L-shaped brick walls connected by a glass-enclosed bridge. Mahogany-clad walls combine with the smaller L to form a volume for service rooms, while glass walls combine with the larger L to create the primary living spaces, which feature southern and western views toward the lake. Entrance is through the larger L-shaped wall and into a space that divides the house into public and private realms.

The entry, living, and sleeping spaces are arranged linearly to maximize lake views and to take advantage of the southern exposure. Large overhangs and sensored motorized shades combine to limit heat gain during the summer while allowing sunlight to penetrate deep into the interior during the winter.

The second-floor roof and exterior walls are wrapped in copper, with fully glazed glass walls inset at the east and west ends of the volume. The glazed wall at the east allows abundant light into the double-height entry hall, while the west end illuminates two bedrooms and offers views of the lake. A single, large punctuation in the southern copper-clad façade provides views from a second-floor office. The sloping roof and canted front wall are designed to deflect fierce north winds and to shed water from intense storms.

Detailing throughout is minimal and precise. The spaces are ordered, and there is a juxtaposition of solidity and transparency. The rigor and linear organization of the design provide an intentionally sharp contrast to the irregular beauty of the landscape.

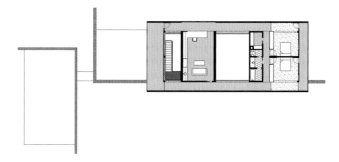

third floor plan

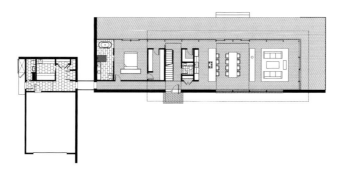

second floor plan

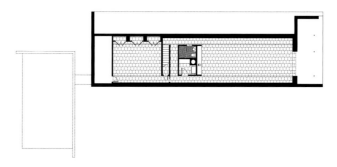

first floor plan

Blue Ridge Farmhouse

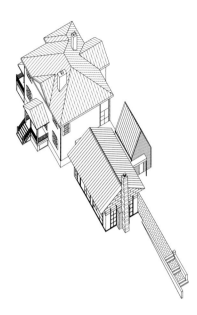

Blue Ridge Farmhouse
Washington, Virginia | 4,590 sq ft | 2003

Comprising gently rolling hills with meandering walls of dry-stacked stone, 500 acres of farmland in central Virginia provide an idyllic setting for this project. A white clapboard farmhouse originally constructed in the late eighteenth century anchors the crest of one hill, providing vantage-point views of the Blue Ridge Mountains. A series of outbuildings, including original service structures for the main farmhouse, remain intact.

The owners desired a space that would bring the outside in while providing views of the landscape and changing seasons. In addition, the owners required a bathroom, closets, and new entry. The new entrance was to provide a threshold to the farmhouse both in a utilitarian and more formal sense.

The unique aspects of this spectacular site and a desire to maintain the integrity of the original house became informative elements in the design of this project. The solution was a careful annexing of elements that respects the existing architecture while avoiding a revivalist or seamless approach. Junctures between old and new are carefully articulated. A transparent glass and steel pavilion provides generous living and entertaining space. The pavilion is conceived as a linear structure with a low-pitched roof that matches the original farmhouse. The horizontal transparency of this pavilion is juxtaposed against the vertical solidity of a white clapboard pavilion with a steeply pitched roof housing a bathroom and closets. These two pavilions combine to frame a new entry. Paved in bluestone, a circulation axis extending from the redefined parking areas continues through the newly framed entry and terminates at an interior stair where a double-height space replaces the old back porch. Along with dry stacked stone and board-formed concrete, this element physically connects the house to the landscape.

The careful juxtaposition of the traditional rural architecture and the new modern pavilions is intended to allow the original farmhouse to remain prominent in the greater composition and serve as a point of reference for the continuing evolution of the site.

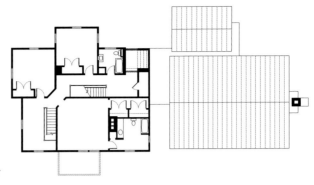

second floor plan after

second floor plan before

first floor plan after

first floor plan before

Hargrave Residence

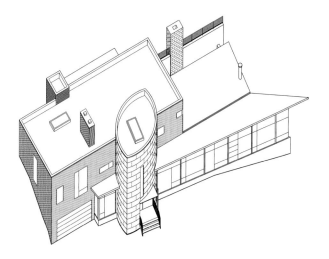

Hargrave Residence Glen Echo, Maryland | 5,500 sq ft | 2003

In a region best known for traditional architecture, Glen Echo, Maryland, stands as an enclave of mid-century modern design. The Hargrave Residence, set on a steeply sloped wooded lot with distant views of the Potomac River, was built partially atop the foundation of a small modern house from the 1950s.

Entry and vertical circulation are through an elliptical tower clad in lead-coated copper. A glass-enclosed living/dining space is topped with an upturned butterfly roof, in response to the sloping topography. The space tapers to a sharp glass triangle that extends into the landscape. A rectangular volume clad in mahogany siding—a remnant of the footprint of the original structure—houses bedroom suites, a fitness room, and a study. Throughout the interior of the house, various woods, steel, glass, aluminum, concrete, and stone combine to create spaces that are diverse, warm, and filled with light.

A terrace with a fireplace is tucked into the hillside adjacent to the living/dining space, increasing connectivity with the outdoors. Bluestone paving and board-formed concrete walls enhance that relationship.

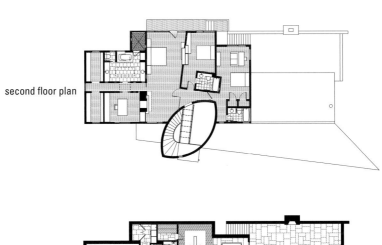

second floor plan

first floor plan

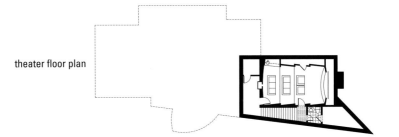

theater floor plan

Georgetown Residence

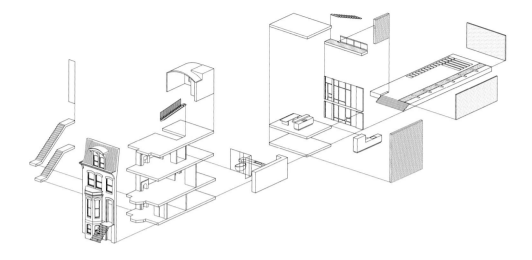

Georgetown Residence Washington, DC | 4,340 sq ft | 2007

This row house in the historic Georgetown district dates from 1876. Constructed in the Second Empire style with Neo-Grec detailing, the house had remained largely unchanged (with the exception of an unsympathetic structure added to the back) until new owners took over with the intent of preserving the historical character but adding modern amenities and space for their expanding art collection.

The entire house was gutted and reconfigured. The main stair at the center of the house was relocated to provide space for a large living room/gallery. A new steel-and-glass addition accommodates a modern kitchen and is visually and physically connected to a new garden. The basement floor was lowered to create additional ceiling height on the ground level, and spaces were rearranged to provide long, open vistas to the garden.

Large rooms with high ceilings, white walls, and recessed lighting were designed to accommodate the owners' art collection. Upstairs, rooms were reconfigured to provide a generous master bedroom suite on the second floor and two bedrooms on the third.

The rooms on the first floor retain the original moldings and detailing. Fireplaces, mantels, and hearths in the living and dining rooms were restored. Interwoven throughout are modern elements; crisply detailed millwork, an open steel stair, stainless steel countertops, and sandblasted glass are juxtaposed with paneled doors and traditional window casings. Dark stained oak floors throughout the house provide a consistent, unifying element.

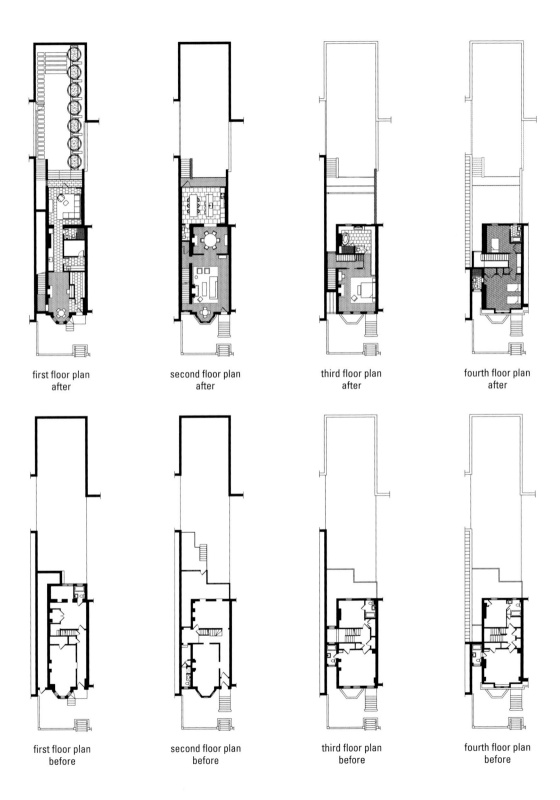

first floor plan
after

second floor plan
after

third floor plan
after

fourth floor plan
after

first floor plan
before

second floor plan
before

third floor plan
before

fourth floor plan
before

Ontario Apartment

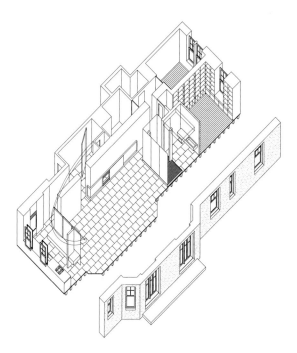

Ontario Apartment Washington, DC | 1,800 sq ft | 2006

This third-floor corner unit of the Ontario—an eight-story, Beaux Arts-inspired 1906 apartment building, with elaborate façades, entry halls, and stairways—had been rendered dim and disorienting by its compartmentalized spaces, dark moldings, and varying wall coverings. The client wished for a renovation that would produce a spare, contemplative urban sanctuary.

The interior was stripped to its essential structure and infrastructure, including existing perimeter walls, column grid, plumbing stacks, and chases. Designed with a formal clarity, the renovated apartment is open and light-filled. Combinations of planar and translucent elements organize and define space. A reductive palette of crisply detailed materials lends a sense of tranquility: Limestone floors, white walls, aluminum, stainless steel, translucent glass, and wenge paneling and cabinetry are used throughout the public areas. In contrast, the bedroom and study employ darkly stained oak flooring and white cabinetry. A curving ceiling plane initiated at the entry fosters spatial unity. Boundaries are blurred by a floating translucent glass volume at one end and three translucent glass panels at the other. The luminous glass allows a subtle awareness of space while creating a sense of mystery. These elements soften the intensity of the natural light, resulting in a serene atmosphere. Furnishings, which reinforce the horizontal planar elements, are integral to the overall composition.

With its turn-of-the-century construction methods and outdated floor plans, the Ontario clearly lends itself to conversion. This project demonstrates how landmark buildings continue to be a viable option for modern urban housing in Washington, DC.

Wissioming Residence

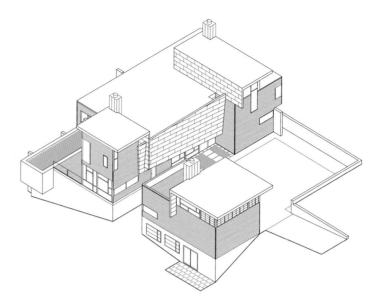

Wissioming Residence
Glen Echo, Maryland | 6,480 sq ft house + 740 sq ft garage | 2007

This house is on a heavily wooded lot overlooking the Potomac River in a suburb of Washington, DC. In order to minimally disturb the site and preserve the mature hardwoods, the project was designed to occupy the footprint of a pre-existing house. A new swimming pool was suspended twenty feet above grade to further reduce the impact on the steeply sloping site.

The owner/builder wanted a home office as part of an effort to lessen his dependence on cars. The office is located on the ground floor of a detached structure—which also contains a garage and upstairs guest suite—separated from the main residence by a reflecting pool. Translucent glass and panels of Kalwall allow the building to serve as a lantern to the main house at night.

Structural pre-cast concrete planks were employed throughout the project in an effort to expedite the construction process; these span large open areas and provide the ability to heat the house hydronically. Large overhangs on the glazed southern wall and the tree canopy minimize solar gain in the summer.

Wood siding is combined with soft gray terne-coated stainless steel and black steel window frames to provide an exterior that fits comfortably in the landscape. Bluestone, gravel, and water complete the materials palette.

Interior materials such as white terrazzo flooring, white oak cabinetry, and aluminum complement the light-filled and minimally detailed space. This atmosphere refocuses the attention outward, allowing visitors to reconnect with the inherently picturesque site.

Sofer Residence

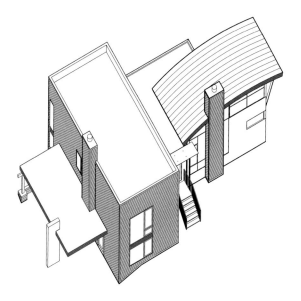

Sofer Residence McLean, Virginia | 2,600 sq ft | 2004

In 1959, 91 houses were built in the Washington, DC, suburb of McLean, Virginia, creating the Lewinsville Heights subdivision. The vast majority of the homes are brick and wood split-levels, sited relatively close to one another and aligned parallel to the street or on axis to the center of a cul-de-sac. The subdivision has remained largely unchanged, except for the maturing landscape.

Each of the 2,100-square-foot split-level houses that occupies this subdivision has a low-pitched roof and an attached carport. The houses are sited with no regard for solar orientation or views and remain isolated from the outdoors. Ceilings are eight feet high, and finishes are simple with typical tract-house detailing.

The owner of this project lived in her split-level for 14 years before deciding to renovate. She desired living spaces that were light-filled and open to her carefully manicured gardens. Her living space was also to serve as a gallery to display her collection of sculptures, mostly by her mother.

The design solution minimally enlarged the existing footprint. In total, only 500 square feet were added to the project. Spatially the house feels substantially enlarged through the in-corporation of expanses of glass and a high, vaulted ceiling floating above large steel windows. New interior detailing is crisp and minimal. A small terrace with wide stairs provides access to the garden.

Light-filled and functional, the renovated house is better connected to the outdoors. The project is also intended to serve as a reminder to the subdivision of the enormous, untapped potential that these prevalent simple houses possess. Primed for renovation, they are viable op-portunities for modern, well-designed houses adaptable to current lifestyle.

northeast elevation after

northeast elevation before

northwest elevation after

northwest elevation before

Windyridge

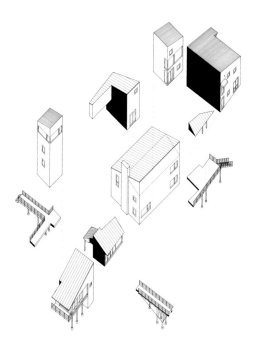

Windyridge

New Creek, West Virginia | 4,200 sq ft | 2000

An ordinary house on an extraordinary site became the starting point for this project. The spectacular lot encompasses 53 acres on top of a mountain in New Creek, West Virginia. The 2,240-square-foot existing house failed to take advantage of breathtaking vistas. The owners bought the property with a vision of a redesigned house organized to capture the incredible views.

To accommodate spatial and programmatic requirements, the house was enlarged to 4,200 square feet, not including a new two-car garage with workspace below. The house was conceived as a village stretched across the top of the mountain. Additional spaces are arranged linearly around the existing house and are rotated toward the optimal view. A narrow, 25-foot-long platform constructed from old bridge parts provides a new entry bridge, extends through the house, and hovers above an existing apple orchard. A four-story observation tower captures panoramic sunset views.

The new scheme includes six volumes painted different colors and clad in different materials, including board and batten, clapboard, and corrugated metal. The volumes are all designed with shed roofs for ease of construction and to simplify water drainage during intense storms.

An acre of mature hardwoods was cleared in an unobtrusive area of the site to yield the black walnut flooring used throughout the house and for the locust ceiling in the new living room. Currently, the owner is cultivating the clearing with specimen bamboo.

The composition of multiple volumes stretching along the ridge provides a variety of spatial experiences. The diversity of forms and textures serves to enrich these experiences.

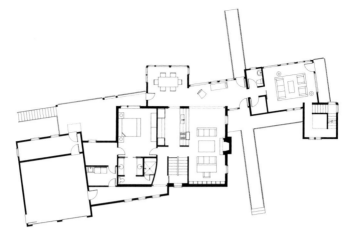

second floor plan after

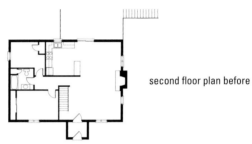

second floor plan before

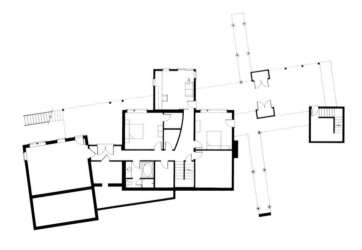

first floor plan after

first floor plan before

Townhouse

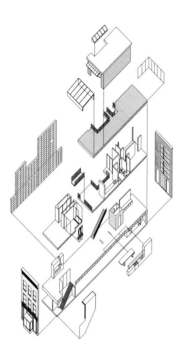

Townhouse   Washington, DC | 4,000 sq ft | 2007

Townhouse was built more than a century ago as part of a continuous network of buildings in a historical district.

The building—an 18- by 100-foot structure that occupies the entire site—was previously used as commercial space on all three floors. Interior spaces were typically dark with nine-foot-high ceilings, the result of a previous renovation.

Regulations required that the traditional limestone facade remain intact. Under the new renovation, the bottom floor of the façade was reworked within the existing limestone composition to provide a separate entrance and storefront for a future commercial tenant on the lower level. The rear facade, located in an alley, was completely reworked to allow light into the building.

The majority of floor joists were retained in an effort to utilize the existing structural system and not disturb the historical facade. To address the redundancy of continuous nine-foot ceilings, a 12-foot-wide section of the third floor was removed. Located directly above this opening, a similar-sized skylight infuses the interior with light. Another section of the third floor was removed to accommodate a stair system. Above the new steel and aluminum stairs, a rooftop addition opens to adjacent terraces and provides outdoor living spaces with rooftop views.

Exposed brick walls were painted white in juxtaposition to blue epoxy floors. Floor openings with bridges, skylights, and a three-story galvanized steel wall animate the spaces and integrate the floors vertically. Glass and steel elements unify a diverse but consistent palette of materials, resulting in a modern spatial quality within a traditional townhouse typology.

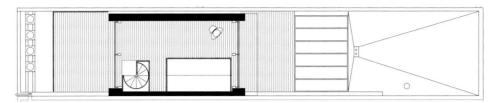

roof deck floor plan

third floor plan

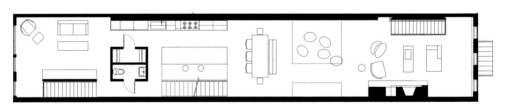

second floor plan

first floor plan

Occoquan River House

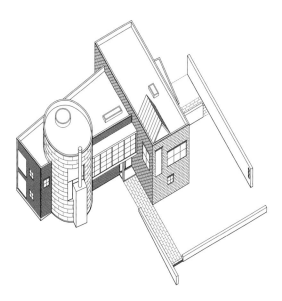

Occoquan River House Occoquan, Virginia | 3,400 sq ft | 2002

This new 3,400-square-foot house is located on five acres of steeply sloping wooded terrain along the Occoquan River in Prince William County, Virginia. The house is placed at the far corner of the site's conservation easement, maximizing the adjacency to the river 60 feet below and obscuring views of a neighboring house. In order to best capture river views, the programmatic section of the house is inverted. Primary living spaces are on the top level, while two bedrooms and two offices are located below, within the privacy of carefully protected existing trees.

The house is conceived as a composition of distinct volumes designed in response to the texture, light, and colors in the landscape. A rectangular volume, constructed with concrete block, embeds the dwelling to the site, while a trapezoidal volume, clad in corrugated metal panels, stretches along the wooded river view and reflects the landscape. A wood and glass structure links the volumes and cantilevers into the landscape. A rotated elliptical cylinder clad in Cor-ten steel anchors the composition and takes on the color of the surrounding earth. Along with the hearth and an offset oculus, this element defines the primary living space. Each volume retains its identity while becoming part of the greater whole. This is most evident where the forms intersect on the second floor. The living, dining, and kitchen spaces are open to each other but are defined by varying ceiling heights and respect the site-specific geometry. The arrangement of spaces and placement of glass allows shifting views of the site and exterior spaces.

With simple forms rendered in sensory materials, the Occoquan River House is part of the larger landscape of river, wood, and sloping site. The constantly shifting environment—fog rolling in off the river, trees changing color, the light of the oculus moving around the living room—creates a rich domestic experience.

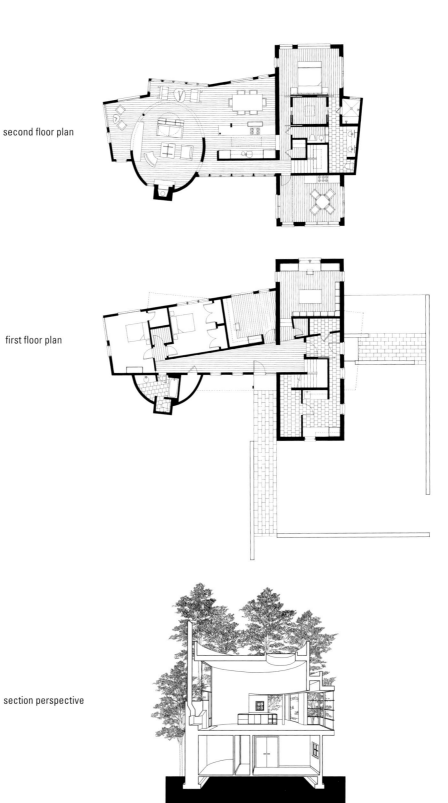

second floor plan

first floor plan

section perspective

Corvasce Goldstein Residence

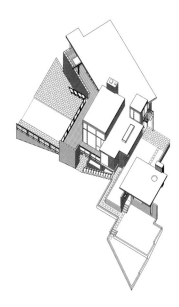

Corvasce Goldstein Residence   Washington, DC | 3,000 sq ft | 2005

This project involved renovating and adding to a mid-century modern house originally designed by noted Washington, DC, architect Chloethiel Woodard Smith. The original kitchen was renovated and other minor changes were implemented in the early 1980s, leaving the majority of the 1950s house intact.

Although the entire house was renovated and enlarged in this latest phase, the transformation is intended to respect the scale and character of the existing house and adjacent mid-century modern houses designed by Walter Gropius.

In the new scheme, a volume was added to clearly define the previously hidden entry. An existing carport was removed and replaced with a new carport that is better sited to further expose the new entry volume. Changes to the interior were more substantial. Spaces were reconfigured, and new finishes were introduced. A low sloping ceiling in the main living space was removed and replaced with a high ceiling and walls of glass that are more appropriate to the scale of the room and provide light-filled spaces open to the outdoors.

New outdoor spaces are accessible from the living areas and incorporate a bluestone terrace, swimming pool, and garden. A series of walls, terraces, and stairs connect and define places throughout the site.

Throughout the project, planar wall elements integrate the house, carport, and landscape. The overall horizontal, low-scaled proportions of the house are maintained. Volumes with high ceilings are carefully organized to minimally impact the horizontal language of this mid-century modern house.

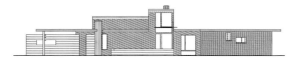

north elevation

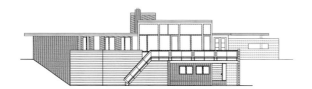

south elevation

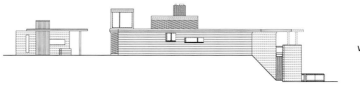

west elevation

east elevation

Peterson Residence

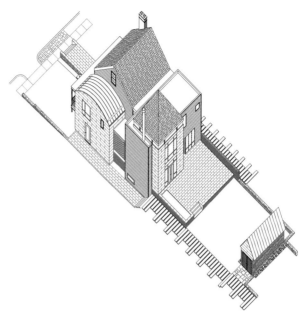

Peterson Residence Chevy Chase, Maryland | 5,300 sq ft | 2007

This project involved a complete renovation and substantial addition to a familiar, simply massed brick colonial-style house. The original, gable-shaped volume fronting the street was kept largely intact, in keeping with the scale and massing of neighboring houses. Tall windows were incorporated into the existing façade.

A copper-clad, vaulted volume was integrated into the composition with a new front porch and wide stairs, invoking the nostalgic porches found throughout the neighborhood. To reduce the massing as seen from the street, the majority of new space was added to the back of the house. Living spaces were relocated to the garden side of the property, away from the street. A new terrace and rigorously designed landscape elements—including walkways, walls, and plantings—became an integral part of the design. A garden structure, constructed of dry-stacked stone, mahogany, steel, and copper roofing, anchors the composition and provides privacy from adjoining properties. The entirety of the lot was incorporated into the design of the project.

The light-filled interiors are ordered and open, crisply detailed, and minimal while retaining richness and warmth. The materials palette includes quarter-sawn white oak cabinetry and millwork, dark-stained oak flooring, mahogany screens, travertine, black granite, and limestone.

Great Falls Residence

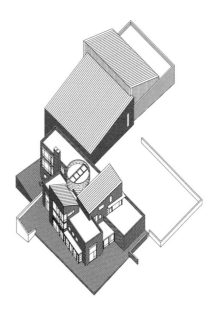

Great Falls Residence
Great Falls, Virginia | 11,000 sq ft house + 8,000 sq ft tennis court | 2004

This house differs immensely from the red brick colonial houses typically built in the surrounding Virginia countryside. The site for this project encompasses 12 acres of sloping topography heavily wooded with mature hardwoods. The strategy was to locate the house on a ridge and take advantage of the most desirable views from a high vantage point.

The house is organized around a 24-foot diameter cylinder clad in Cor-ten steel. This cylinder contains the stairs and a series of bridges, which connect spaces in different volumes. Two linear, ground-faced block volumes engage the cylinder; one of the volumes is rotated 10 degrees toward the optimal views. A pair of shed-roofed structures, clad in corrugated Galvalume, emerge from the ground-faced block volumes.

The clients requested an indoor tennis court visible from the living space inside the main house. The tennis court occupies 8,000 square feet and is 40 feet high at the net. This is a large structure, even on the 12-acre site. The tennis court is set into the heavily wooded hillside to reduce its visibility and is sited so that, from inside the main house, it is visible only from a viewing space adjacent to the main living room. The tennis court structure employs sloping shed roofs and similar materials to those on the main house.

Materials chosen for this project provide for a house that fits comfortably into its wooded environment and will not require extended maintenance. The ground-faced block and Galvalume are soft grey in color, similar to the bark on adjacent trees. The Cor-ten steel is reddish brown and is constantly changing in color, similar to the surrounding landscape. Concrete retaining walls and bluestone terraces continue the palette of materials that are harmonious with the landscape.

Jacobson Guesthouse

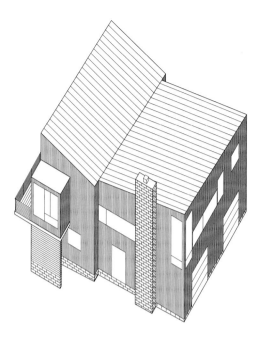

Jacobson Guesthouse Mineral, Virginia | 2,835 sq ft | 2007

As the first phase of a client's planned move to Lake Anna near Mineral, Virginia, this guesthouse and garage became the starting point for further development of the site.

The design set a precedent of economy. Simple methods of construction allowed the client to build the house himself, enabling him to familiarize himself with the timeless materials—such as concrete block and rusted, corrugated metal siding—for better efficiency and ease of maintenance in the future.

The processes of design and construction became a constant exchange between client and architect, as they experimented with materials and developed methods that satisfied both parties' desires for composition, functionality, and longevity.

The living spaces were designed to be light-filled and generous. Plywood, off-the-shelf millwork, cement board panels, and porcelain tile bring the richness of the exterior inside.

Duncan Residence

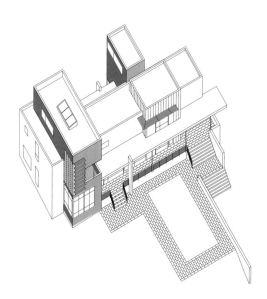

Duncan Residence Annapolis, Maryland | 3,420 sq ft | 2007

Situated near Crab Creek, an estuary that feeds Chesapeake Bay, this project was built on the foundation of a 1960s post-and-beam modern house, as strict environmental regulations prohibited enlarging the pre-existing footprint or adding significant square footage.

The house is organized around a linear bar, clad in white stucco. From this central spine, additional spaces are articulated as independent volumes, projecting vertically and clad in either wood or metal siding. The spaces are also organized around a swimming pool and views toward Crab Creek. A continuous wall of glass and a covered porch heighten the interaction between indoors and outdoors. Additional materials used on the exterior include field stone, board-formed concrete, bluestone, and ground-faced block.

Inside, the primary spaces are oriented toward water views, have high ceilings, and are filled with light. Materials used throughout the interior include white oak flooring and millwork, black slate, white marble, rusted steel, and translucent glass.

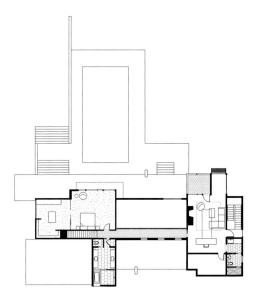

second floor plan

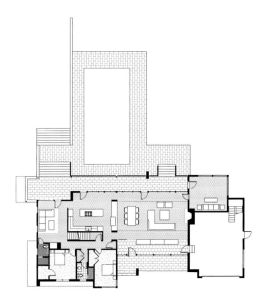

first floor plan

Packard Komoriya Residence

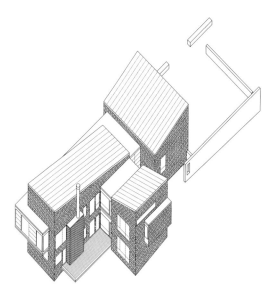

Packard Komoriya Residence Potomac, Maryland | 4,000 sq ft | 2004

This new house was designed and sited to preserve the natural features of a sloping, wooded landscape and to maximize views of horse fields and the heavily wooded, rolling topography adjacent to the site.

The owners have been significantly influenced by their ties to Japan and their exposure to that country's meticulously crafted wood structures. They share the Japanese reverence for wood, aesthetically and structurally. They wanted their new house to draw reference from Japanese architecture without imitation.

The 4,000-square-foot house is composed of three structures with simple shed roofs organized to fit unobtrusively into the landscape. These volumes are clad in cedar shingles and help articulate the craft of building. Flat-roofed, glass-walled structures, intended to feel like bridges, connect the three volumes. Dry-stacked stone walls and board-formed concrete walls are designed to fit with the rugged rock outcroppings found throughout the site. Materials used on the interior include bluestone in the entry area and Brazilian cherry flooring throughout the remainder of the house. Maple cabinetry, millwork, and paneling enrich the spaces.

Stone and wood, articulated in various elements and surfaces throughout the project, unify this house and the site, allowing the inhabitants to better enjoy the surrounding landscape.

north elevation

east elevation

south elevation

west elevation

Fitch O'Rourke Residence

Fitch O'Rourke Residence Washington, DC | 4,000 sq ft | 2000

Located in Washington's Kalorama/Adams Morgan neighborhood, this townhouse was considered an eyesore for many years. The previous owner had gutted the interior and demolished the entire back wall of the townhouse before a zoning dispute stopped his effort to convert it into a multi-unit condominium. For the next several years, the building shell remained in this broken-down condition, filled with debris, completely open to outdoor conditions.

The new owners viewed the property as a rare opportunity to build a completely new, modern residence in an established in-town neighborhood. Their program included a two-bedroom, two-study residence (convertible to three bedrooms and one study) on the upper three levels, and a one-bedroom rental unit in the basement. They wanted a warm, intimate, and dynamic home that responded to its urban location.

The project faced three serious constraints: the house's long, narrow footprint (63 feet long, about 17 feet wide on the front, narrowing to 13 feet); the property's location in a designated historic district, which required the front façade to be kept intact; and the clients' limited budget.

The design for the project transcends the building's narrow confines by combining a traditional orthogonal scheme with a curving geometry (where most curves and radials trace back to a center point 28 feet east of the house) and a rotation space (based on a 10-degree diagonal running from a rear corner to the center of the dining room). The resulting arrangement moves and changes as one navigates through the house.

The living room exploits the southern exposure and the opportunity to build a new rear façade that could bring light into a lofted space. A second lofted area near the front brings light into the northern end. Primary materials were chosen to create a rich and warm mix of colors and textures that admit and modulate light, responding to the urban context.

basement
floor plan

first floor
plan

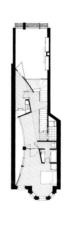

second floor
plan

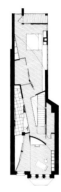

third floor
plan

Ten Year House

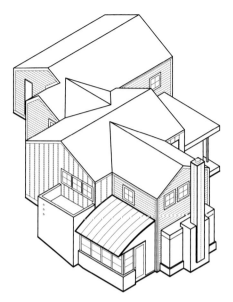

Ten Year House   Bethesda, Maryland | 2,480 sq ft | 2006

Constructed over a ten-year period, this project was a collaboration between Robert Gurney and an architectural photographer with whom he had a longtime working relationship.

The house is located on a wooded lot in a very desirable neighborhood outside Washington, DC. The original two-story structure was constructed in 1906 and comprised about 1,100 square feet, with seven-foot-high ceilings on the main floor. Two small additions were added in the 1950s, and a larger addition was added in 1980; together, these doubled the size of the house.

The client purchased the house with the intention of renovating it over time as resources would allow, to create an open, light-filled structure with views to the wooded surroundings.

Due to the very tight budget, most of the house's original massing and structure were kept intact–in all, only 165 square feet were added. The majority of changes involved reconfiguring the small, single-function rooms into a cohesive, open floor plan and altering ceiling heights within the existing volumes. Large expanses of glass were added. Ultimately, all the spaces in the house were gutted and received new finishes.

Deviation from the original master plan was minimal over the lengthy construction period. Materials and finishes changed but were always chosen to be compatible with previous selections.

The completed project is a holistic, singular representation of the client's original goals. This project represents an unconventional but successful approach to renovation, in which patience and perseverance can replace abundant resources and the desire for instant gratification.

Kessler Residence

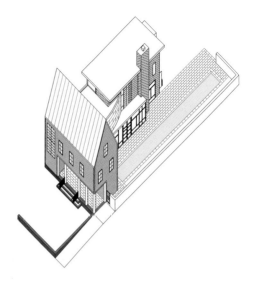

Kessler Residence Chevy Chase, Maryland | 3,800 sq ft | 2004

An empty side yard of an existing house became the lot for this new project in a neighborhood of homes built during the romantic period of domestic architecture. While intent on preserving the intimate atmosphere of the neighborhood, the clients, a young couple with twin daughters, wanted a modern house conducive to their casual lifestyle. They desired a light-filled, open floor plan with a variety of generous yet intimately scaled spaces, with no underused, formal living or dining rooms. Additionally, the house was to be universally designed to accommodate one daughter's disabilities.

The 3,800-square-foot house is organized around a 75-foot-long lap pool. The linear arrangement and orientation of spaces are governed by the narrow lot, which is 50 feet wide and 150 feet deep. The major living spaces open to the pool and the southern exposure. Views of a neighboring house to the west are shielded through the careful placement of windows and translucent panels.

Open spaces, wide halls, and an elevator allow the disabled daughter easy access to any part of the house. Fully accessible bathrooms, the kitchen, and the pool were designed to minimize her dependence on a wheelchair.

Simple lines and natural materials relate the house to its neighborhood. A two-story, 18-foot-deep by 36-foot-long volume with a steeply pitched roof serves as a threshold between the historic context and the modernist house. A front porch with columns continues the rhythm of neighboring homes. The abstraction of familiar elements—columns, clapboard siding, standing seam metal roof, brick base, and bluestone porch—preserves the historic character and domestic scale of the street.

east elevation

south elevation

west elevation

north elevation

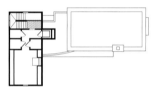

third floor plan

second floor plan

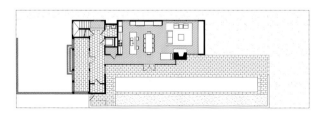

first floor plan

Credits

Blue Ridge Farmhouse
Washington, Virginia
YEAR COMPLETED: 2003
DESIGN PRINCIPAL: Robert M. Gurney, FAIA
PROJECT ARCHITECT: Hito Martinez
STRUCTURAL ENGINEER: D. Anthony Beale, PE, SE
GENERAL CONTRACTOR: M.T. Puskar Construction Company, Inc.
INTERIOR DESIGNER: Ed Perlman
PHOTOGRAPHY: Paul Warchol,
except Ken Gutmaker, page 29 (top)

Buisson Residence
Lake Anna, Virginia
YEAR COMPLETED: 2008
DESIGN PRINCIPAL: Robert M. Gurney, FAIA
PROJECT ARCHITECT: Claire L. Andreas
STRUCTURAL ENGINEER: D. Anthony Beale, PE, SE
GENERAL CONTRACTOR: Loudin Building Systems
INTERIOR DESIGNER: Thérèse Baron Gurney, ASID
OWNERS: James and Nora Buisson
PHOTOGRAPHY: Maxwell MacKenzie,
except Paul Warchol, pages 10-11 and 21 (top)

Corvasce Goldstein Residence
Washington, DC
YEAR COMPLETED: 2005
DESIGN PRINCIPAL: Robert M. Gurney, FAIA
PROJECT ARCHITECT: Hito Martinez
STRUCTURAL ENGINEER: D. Anthony Beale, PE, SE
GENERAL CONTRACTOR: Prill Construction
INTERIOR DESIGNER: Thérèse Baron Gurney, ASID
OWNERS: Antonietta Corvasce and Stephen Goldstein
PHOTOGRAPHY: Anice Hoachlander

Duncan Residence
Annapolis, Maryland
YEAR COMPLETED: 2007
DESIGN PRINCIPAL: Robert M. Gurney, FAIA
PROJECT ARCHITECT: Brian Tuskey
STRUCTURAL ENGINEER: D. Anthony Beale, PE, SE
OWNERS: Mary and Steve Duncan
PHOTOGRAPHY: Anice Hoachlander

Fitch O'Rourke Residence
Washington, DC
YEAR COMPLETED: 2000
DESIGN PRINCIPAL: Robert M. Gurney, FAIA
PROJECT ARCHITECT: Hito Martinez
STRUCTURAL ENGINEER: D. Anthony Beale, PE, SE
INTERIOR DESIGNER: Thérèse Baron Gurney, ASID
OWNERS: Mary Fitch and Ron O'Rourke
PHOTOGRAPHY: Paul Warchol

Georgetown Residence

Washington, DC

YEAR COMPLETED: 2007

DESIGN PRINCIPAL: Robert M. Gurney, FAIA

PROJECT ARCHITECT: Claire L. Andreas

STRUCTURAL ENGINEER: D. Anthony Beale, PE, SE

GENERAL CONTRACTOR: Prill Construction

INTERIOR DESIGNER: Thérèse Baron Gurney, ASID

PHOTOGRAPHY: Maxwell MacKenzie

Great Falls Residence

Great Falls, Virginia

YEAR COMPLETED: 2004

DESIGN PRINCIPAL: Robert M. Gurney, FAIA

PROJECT ARCHITECT: Benjamin Ames

STRUCTURAL ENGINEER: D. Anthony Beale, PE, SE

GENERAL CONTRACTOR: SugarOak Corporation

PHOTOGRAPHY: Anice Hoachlander

Hargrave Residence

Glen Echo, Maryland

YEAR COMPLETED: 2003

DESIGN PRINCIPAL: Robert M. Gurney, FAIA

PROJECT ARCHITECT: Claire L. Andreas

STRUCTURAL ENGINEER: D. Anthony Beale, PE, SE

GENERAL CONTRACTOR: M.T. Puskar Construction Company, Inc.

INTERIOR DESIGNER: Thérèse Baron Gurney, ASID

OWNER: Ken Hargrave

PHOTOGRAPHY: Anice Hoachlander

Jacobson Guesthouse

Mineral, Virginia

YEAR COMPLETED: 2007

DESIGN PRINCIPAL: Robert M. Gurney, FAIA

PROJECT ARCHITECT: Brian Tuskey

STRUCTURAL ENGINEER: D. Anthony Beale, PE, SE

OWNER: Michael Jacobson

PHOTOGRAPHY: Anice Hoachlander

Kessler Residence

Chevy Chase, Maryland

YEAR COMPLETED: 2004

DESIGN PRINCIPAL: Robert M. Gurney, FAIA

STRUCTURAL ENGINEER: D. Anthony Beale, PE, SE

GENERAL CONTRACTOR: M.T. Puskar Construction Company, Inc.

OWNERS: Lewis and Tamara Kessler

PHOTOGRAPHY: Maxwell MacKenzie

Occoquan River House

Occoquan, Virginia

YEAR COMPLETED: 2002

DESIGN PRINCIPAL: Robert M. Gurney, FAIA

STRUCTURAL ENGINEER: D. Anthony Beale, PE, SE

GENERAL CONTRACTOR: Chandler Construction, Inc.

INTERIOR DESIGNER: Thérèse Baron Gurney, ASID

OWNERS: Joanne Lindenberger and Benjamin Schutz

PHOTOGRAPHER: Anice Hoachlander, except Paul Warchol, page 90

Ontario Apartment

Washington, DC

YEAR COMPLETED: 2006

DESIGN PRINCIPAL: Robert M. Gurney, FAIA

PROJECT ARCHITECT: Brian Tuskey

STRUCTURAL ENGINEER: D. Anthony Beale, PE, SE

GENERAL CONTRACTOR: Added Dimensions, Inc.

INTERIOR DESIGNER: Thérèse Baron Gurney, ASID

PHOTOGRAPHY: Maxwell MacKenzie

Packard Komoriya Residence

Potomac, Maryland

YEAR COMPLETED: 2004

DESIGN PRINCIPAL: Robert M. Gurney, FAIA

STRUCTURAL ENGINEER: D. Anthony Beale, PE, SE

GENERAL CONTRACTOR: O.C. Builders, Inc.

OWNERS: Akira Komoriya and Beverly Packard

PHOTOGRAPHY: Anice Hoachlander

Peterson Residence

Chevy Chase, Maryland
YEAR COMPLETED: 2007
DESIGN PRINCIPAL: Robert M. Gurney, FAIA
PROJECT ARCHITECT: Claire L. Andreas
STRUCTURAL ENGINEER: D. Anthony Beale, PE, SE
GENERAL CONTRACTOR: Peterson and Collins, Inc.
INTERIOR DESIGNER: Thérèse Baron Gurney, ASID
OWNERS: Ted and Tish Peterson
PHOTOGRAPHY: Maxwell MacKenzie

Sofer Residence

McLean, Virginia
YEAR COMPLETED: 2004
DESIGN PRINCIPAL: Robert M. Gurney, FAIA
PROJECT ARCHITECT: Hito Martinez
STRUCTURAL ENGINEER: D. Anthony Beale, PE, SE
INTERIOR DESIGNER: Thérèse Baron Gurney, ASID
OWNERS: Ariela Sofer
PHOTOGRAPHY: Anice Hoachlander

Ten Year House

Bethesda, Maryland
YEAR COMPLETED: 2006
DESIGN PRINCIPAL: Robert M. Gurney, FAIA
STRUCTURAL ENGINEER: D. Anthony Beale, PE, SE
INTERIOR DESIGNER: Thérèse Baron Gurney, ASID
OWNERS: Anice Hoachlander and Peter Hobby
PHOTOGRAPHY: Anice Hoachlander

Townhouse

Washington, DC
YEAR COMPLETED: 2007
DESIGN PRINCIPAL: Robert M. Gurney, FAIA
PROJECT ARCHITECT: John Riordan
STRUCTURAL ENGINEER: D. Anthony Beale, PE, SE
GENERAL CONTRACTOR: Prill Construction
OWNERS: Max and Katie Brown
PHOTOGRAPHY: Paul Warchol

Windyridge

New Creek, West Virginia
YEAR COMPLETED: 2000
DESIGN PRINCIPAL: Robert M. Gurney, FAIA
PROJECT ARCHITECTS: Hito Martinez
STRUCTURAL ENGINEER: D. Anthony Beale, PE, SE
GENERAL CONTRACTOR: Quality Homes
OWNERS: Twila and Wayne Engle
PHOTOGRAPHY: Anice Hoachlander

Wissioming Residence

Glen Echo, Maryland
YEAR COMPLETED: 2007
DESIGN PRINCIPAL: Robert M. Gurney, FAIA
PROJECT ARCHITECT: Brian Tuskey
STRUCTURAL ENGINEER: D. Anthony Beale, PE, SE
GENERAL CONTRACTOR: Bloom Builders
INTERIOR DESIGNER: Thérèse Baron Gurney, ASID
OWNERS: Lewie Bloom and Nancy Schwartz
PHOTOGRAPHY: Maxwell MacKenzie

Acknowledgments

Seeing projects built is the reward and culmination of the time, effort, commitment, patience, and perseverance of many people. Clients provide the challenge, faith, and financial resources—and they often lend insight. Many become friends. The builders and craftsman with whom I have been fortunate enough to work have my respect and gratitude; I have learned more from them than they have from me. In addition, the talented and dedicated professionals in my office have contributed immensely. I am especially grateful to Hito Martinez, Claire Andreas, Brian Tuskey, Sarah Mailhot, and John Riordan.

Thanks to my parents, Robert and Irene Gurney, who provided me with all the tools and support necessary to pursue my passion.

I am most grateful to my children, Robert and Alyson, and my wife, Thérèse, for their patience, love, wisdom, and support. They have looked at more buildings than have most architecture critics. Robert's creativity and energy are contagious. Alyson has become my computer consultant when I work at home. Thérèse has provided unwavering support and afforded me every opportunity to immerse myself in this profession. She is greatly responsible for the interiors of all the projects and solely responsible for the interiors of many. All the work is better because of her.

–Robert Gurney